IMAGES
of England

WHITEHAVEN

Private Acton VC. Abraham Acton was born in 1892 and died 16 May 1915. He was born at No. 2 Tysons Court, adjacent to Roper Street. He attended Crosthwaite School, Rosemary Lane from 10 May 1899 to April 1906. Private Acton was awarded a posthumous VC for his valiant efforts to rescue colleagues in the face of enemy gunfire during the First World War. Private Acton was mortally wounded in action at the age of 22. He was one of just ten Border Regiment soldiers to have won Britain's highest military honour.

The swing bridge was used to carry coal wagons across the docks, seen here c. 1913. The shipyards stood to the left of the picture and a swing bridge was necessary to allow ships access when required.

This scene illustrates how busy the harbour has become, with buildings packed around the quays, c. 1900.

Fishing boats are tied up at the old quay, *c.* 1905. There is plenty of smoke from William Pit in the background.

West Pier. Nets are laid out along the south pier near Wellington beach.

Sugar Tongue, *c.* 1910. This is where the *Cumberland* used to land her cargo, later it appeared to be devoted solely to the shipment of iron ore.

West Strand tides, showing the harbour at high tide. The water is receding here but obviously the whole area was often flooded.

The piers. Boats are leaving the harbour on the high tide.

East Strand, pre-1900. The notice on the wall refers to Joesph Moore who was listed as a carter in George Street, in 1873. This was a branch office of Whitehaven Cab and General Company Ltd.

A coal hurry on the north pier, c. 1907.

The lock-gate keeper stands by the capstan at the Queens docks.

Harbour side. Wellington Pit and West Strand are pictured during slum clearance, c. 1970. The Beacon now occupies this site.

Pow Beck, West Strand. From Preston Street and beyond, Pow Beck flows through Market Place to the harbour. Now completely covered over it was an open beck with bridges across in the seventeenth century. It is pictured during alterations in 1927. The arch dates from 1730 and is 9 feet wide. The water passes down ten steps at this point and flows into the harbour at west strand.

A horse pulls a chaldron wagon from the staithe, c. 1910. Pattinson mill stands on the right.

North Beach, Whitehaven. This view shows Lord Lonsdale ironworks at the top left, with William Pit on the left below Bransty.

A group of Victorian ladies are pictured at a reception aboard the *Eleanor Dixon* in 1860.

Five
Coal Mining and Mines

*Christopher Lowther was a merchant in Dublin when he acquired the Whitehaven estate around 1630.
The land contained good quality coal seams, which were already being utilised by digging the coal from
the surface. Coal was worked from the outcrops or exposed seams so no machinery was necessary.
Some of these places were known as Bear Mouths, men dug out the coal and the women and children
carried it out on their backs. Investment was later made into machinery and several deep mines were
sunk and developed; a number of books in The Beacon expand on this development. This illustrative
selection will hopefully whet the reader's appetite.*

Newcomen engine. The first steam engine to be used to pump water from the pit was erected
by James Lowther at Stone Pit Ginns. The agreement is dated 10 November 1715.

Saltom Pit. This was the first deep mine to go under the sea, it was sunk in an oval shape. It was the deepest pit in the country at that time; 1729-1848. The Newcomen engine was used here.

Ladysmith Pit. The sinking of the pit took place in 1902. Croft Pit is on the left and was worked from 1902 to 1933.

William Pit. This was described as the most dangerous pit in the country. Although work started on this pit in 1806 it was not until 1812 that it was fully operational. Methane gas made these mines dangerous and many disasters occurred, the worst one being on 15 August 1947 when 104 miners lost their lives. This pit remained open until 1955.

Wellington Pit. This pit was built with castellations and turrets in order to resemble a castle and thereby enhance the area and reflect the wealth of the Lowther family. The pit was sunk on the southern shore of the harbour. Methane gas was again the culprit when an explosion on 11 May 1910 caused the loss of 137 men's lives.

Duke Pit. The picture shows the remains of the fan house and ventilation shaft. The first shaft was sunk in 1747 by Carlisle Spedding, the second shaft was sunk by John Peile 1819.

Haig Pit. Sunk between 1916 and 1918, the pit was closed in 1986; it was the last deep coal mine in Cumbria. There are now plans to make the area into a mining museum.

Howgill Brake. Coal wagons are pictured at the bottom of the brake on South Shore.

Wagons traverse the track from the brake round the harbour to marshalling yards behind William Pit on the North Shore.

Wellington Pit rescuers are ready to descend. The men are pictured on the surface following the disaster of May 1910.

William Pit rescue team.

Funeral cortege for some of the miners killed in the Wellington Pit disaster of 1910. So many miners were killed that mass funerals had to take place.

Saltom Brows. Men and boys are hewing coal during the 1912 strike.

Candlestick chimney. This was built to release the methane gas from the pit. It was supposedly built to the same design as the candlesticks in Whitehaven Castle and the Lowther crest is engraved on the side. When it was first completed there was a large six foot flame-shaped extension, which was later taken down as it was deemed to be dangerous.
Occasionally during a thunderstorm the candlestick would be ignited due to the methane gas building up inside.

'Seldom Seen' Greenbank, the site of a seventeenth-century coalmine, c. 1920. The cottage was demolished in 1938. Seated outside is Mr G. Beck, the great-grandfather of Alistair Bullock.

Six

Market Place

A market charter was granted to Whitehaven in 1654 and confirmed in 1660. There was a building on this site which was rebuilt and opened on 1 January 1819. It was designed by Sir Robert Smirke and was known as a butter market. In the 1880s the original building was demolished and the present building erected to a design by T. Linneas Banks, it opened on 2 June 1881. At this time the ground floor was used as a market, while the upper floors were used for a variety of purposes. Since 1881 the upper floors have been used as a dance hall, for meetings, as one of the first venues to show films in the 1900s, as a billiard hall, pram warehouse, tie factory and as an electrical wholesalers. In the 1920s the market hall was used as an unemployment benefit office due to the depression. After refurbishment in 1974 the building was occupied by the newly formed Whitehaven Museum and the Tourist Information centre. In 1986 the building was found to be unsafe and the museum moved into the civic hall. After extensive repairs the building was opened once again in 1994, with the Tourist Information centre situated on the ground floor. The rest of the building is occupied by the Whitehaven Development Company and the restaurant on the upper floor is run by the Whitehaven Youth Trust.

The first market hall was opened on 1 January 1819 and was demolished in 1880.

The market hall, nearly twenty-five years later, *c.* 1905. The cocoa rooms are to the right of the picture.

A flooded Market Place, *c.* 1900. The floods were caused by a combination of high tides, rough weather and the Pow Beck being swollen by rain. Such intrusions usually receded after an hour, when the tide ebbed, but invariably a great deal of damage would have been caused.

Walter Willson's grocery shop in Market Place. Butter is 5p per lb. Notice the sides of bacon hanging outside, health regulations would not allow this today.

Sub-post office, Reynolds and Naile. There has been a post office on this site since the late nineteenth century and it is still run as a post office today by Mr J. McDowell. The newspaper, dated 26 May 1900, shows the relief of Mafeking. A chemist has occupied the premises next door since 1898.

Leech Furnishing Stores at No. 58 Market Place appear to stock everything. There is a dolly tub, a posser and a pram in the doorway, *c.* 1900.

A lady sorts out her wares ready for the market, from a barrow supported across two barrels, *c.* 1904.

Green Market with the iron stobs, *c.* 1905. The area contained by the stobs was for the sole use of the Lowther Estates products. Dalzells shop at No. 41 King Street and the Golden Lion Hotel can be seen. The street between these buildings is Roper Street.

This young man shepherds a flock of sheep through the market, *c.* 1862. Roan's shop and the refuge school can be seen in the background.

The Newtown end of Market Place. On the right is Roan's furniture shop; the dark passageway leads to the Old Town and Swingpump Lane. Just off Swingpump Lane is Ribton Lane.

The eastern side of Swingpump Lane. The shop doorway on the right was Christine's pram shop, the picture demonstrates how narrow the streets were.

Swingpump Lane behind the Market Place was named after the swingpump which was situated here. On the extreme left is the Pineapple public house.

Dusty Miller public house.

Ribton Lane. This was the site of the factory which later became Marchon, and is now Albright and Wilson. It was a firelighter factory occupying an old-run down building. Firelighters were made by packing wood shavings into four small sticks fastened with wire and then dipping them into flammable material. The factory burnt down in the 1950s. The Beacon has now acquired the machine that was used for this process. Marchon was an amalgamation of the founders' names; Mr Schon and Mr Marzillier.

A further view of the firelighter factory. Rosemary Lane is in the background.

New steps leading from Ribton Lane to Rosemary Lane. They were 'new' in the late 1800s.

View from Rosemary Lane, *c.* 1958. Hogarth Mission is on the left of the picture. Rosemary Lane was so called because of the profusion of rosemary that grew there when Mount Pleasant was a garden belonging to the Wybergs in the seventeenth century.

Hogarth House, *c.* 1950. Revd James Hogarth lived here. The houses were demolished in the 1960s.

Seven

New Houses, Newtown and Preston Street

As Whitehaven developed and the population increased more housing was needed. Because of the grid iron plan it was impossible to extend outwards, so many of the houses were built behind the larger mansions. Much of this infill caused serious overcrowding and squalor. In 1788 Lord Lowther built three rows of houses above Preston Street into the Brows. These were small houses, one up one down, and were built one row above another with the front doors opening out to the roof below. There was no water or sanitation and this caused great hardship and disease, though these houses were better than the hovels the occupants had left behind in the rural areas at that time. They were built to accommodate miners coming to Whitehaven to work in the Lowther mines, so were in effect tied cottages.

Newtown leading off Market Place towards Preston Street, c. 1910. Notice the railway lines, which brought goods from the harbour to the goods yards in Preston Street.

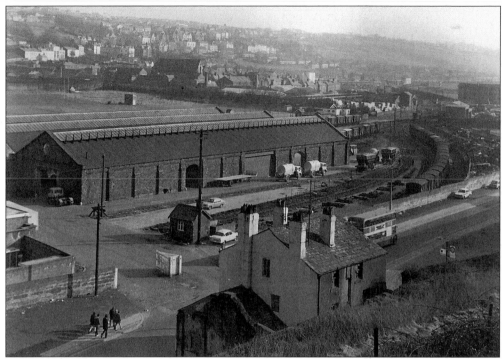

A view of the goods depot in Preston Street, from Rosemary Lane.

These cottages are situated at the start of Preston Street, opposite the goods yard, *c.* 1950. New Houses were built behind and above these.

Looking over Newtown from the Brows at the wider area of Whitehaven, 1930s. This shows just how congested the town had become.

Stout's Foundry, Newtown. This was demolished in 1997.

Christ Church temporary rooms in the 1950s. This was the original old pit engine house at the far end of Preston Street, towards Coach Road.

New Houses. Lavatories had been added by this time; one lavatory and one tap was shared between eight houses. The rent was 5s 6d per week.

By this time efforts had been made to modernise these houses. Each group of three houses was converted into two. The ground floor room of the middle house was added to the first house, while the bedroom was added to the third house, so the middle house disappeared. Great efforts were made to keep them clean; they were whitewashed inside and out regularly, but the population was too large and the amenities too few to make them really habitable; they were demolished in the late 1930s.

The middle row of New Houses contained a building designed like a small church. It is said to have been a small, six-bed hospital where any injured miners were brought after accidents in the pits.

Newtown. Picured is the end of a row of terraced houses in Preston Street, below the New Houses, a prime example of houses in the Newtown area. These were situated next to a large warehouse which was owned by Knowles and Fidler Ltd. Later it was used as the West Cumberland Farmers grain warehouse. These houses were demolished in the late 1950s.

Eight
Roper Street

Roper Street is one of the earliest streets to exist in Whitehaven and was probably named after Ceasor Barnes the roper, who lived at No. 51, which later became the Indian King public house. The tenancy of this pub dates back to at least 1663 and has links with Sandhills Lane. Rope Walks House can still be seen, it is now shop selling electrical goods. No. 10, the Royal Hotel, dates back to 1667.

R. Brew's clogger's shop. This building dates back to the seventeenth century. Hand-made clogs were fashioned here until the 1970s. Further down is Thomas Whittle and Graham ironmongers which closed in the 1990s. The building with furniture written along the side was formerly Ennerdale Aerated Water Co., bottlers of mineral water, Bass ales and Guinness stout. This factory stretches back to Queen Street.

Shakespeare public house is decorated in celebration of the coronation of George V, 1911. Note the proportions of the building.

The Old Theatre Royal. This dates back to 1769. In the archives at The Beacon there is a poster advertising a performance on the 22 November. The theatre was closed for refurbishment and reopened on 1 February 1869. It was remodelled once again in 1909, then closed in the 1930s and was finally demolished in the 1960s. Extensions to the printing works were built on the site which was later used by Micheal Moon for his antiquarian book shop. He has now moved his premises to Lowther Street.

The left hand balcony box at the Old
Theatre, pictured during demolition.

Theatre boxes to the left of the stage.

Roper Street's north-eastern side in the 1970s, before restoration work started. Singleton's shop is at the end of the row.

Stout's warehouse, now converted into flats.

No. 30 Roper Street, home and office to the Spedding's, agent to the Lowther family. The warehouse, the building seen in the previous picture, belonged to the Speddings. The other doorway into the house was on the Scotch Street side.

William Winter; grocer, tea dealer and provisions merchant.

Nos 23 and 24 Roper Street; these houses are virtually mirror images of each other. They were built in 1738 by Joseph Hind and Bernard Swainson. Bernard Swainson died soon afterwards, heavily in debt as the result of financing the construction of such a fine house and stables.

A bow window on the south-western side of Roper Street.

Nine
Scotch Street

Scotch Street is of a later date than the other streets seen so far. It is an extension of Irish Street, which stretches from the Newtown area to the junction with High Street. There is no evidence to show why the streets were so called, it may be because of the trade links with Scotland and Ireland.

Holy Trinity church, in Scotch Street, was built in 1714-15 and consecrated by the Bishop of Chester on 2 October 1715. The church was demolished in 1949 and the gravestones were moved to the walls. The area was landscaped with a raised garden for the disabled; it is a lovely, secluded garden to visit.

No. 14 Scotch Street was occupied in 1829 by Isaac Littledale. He ran for parliament in 1832 but lost to Matthias Attwood. There has been a house on this site since 1738 but it must have been altered in the Georgian era, *c.* 1830. The doorway is of classic proportions with a triangular pediment above and there is a stone balustrade running the length of the house. The property has recently been restored and now belongs to Bleasdale solicitors.

Scotch Street, outside the Trinity church area, looking towards the tannery, *c.* 1900. The Methodist church on the right of the picture was built in 1879. Beyond this is the Congregational church, built in 1875.

These cottages, at the rear of the police station in Scotch Street, were demolished in the 1950s. These were functional buildings compared to merchant's houses.

View towards the tannery, from Duke Street, c. 1907. Walker's shop is on the right, with the tannery and chimney at the top of the picture.

Upper Scotch Street houses, *c.* 1950. New Star Hotel is on the right. This view shows how steep the hill is.

The northern end of Scotch Street, *c.* 1961. The larger building may have been a warehouse. The steep incline of the hill is again well illustrated.

No. 109 Scotch Street. The Lowther's plot was purchased by Carlisle Spedding, their colliery agent, in 1716.

Upper Scotch Street, in 1958. The buildings on the western side were demolished in 1958. Now there is a block of flats on the site. Here we see the walkway between the tan yard buildings.

Nos 1 to 5 Union Terrace, Scotch Street, by the tannery. These were small houses (one-up, one-down), built for the workers, which were demolished during the slum clearance of the 1950s and '60s.

74

Upper Scotch Street, at the rear of the old tannery. By the 1960s, this area had been completely cleared.

This view of the old tannery buildings looks down Scotch Street towards Irish Street.

The tannery, Scotch Street. After closure it was sold on 10 April 1958. St James church stands in the background.

Messrs Walkers' tan yard at Whitehaven. It was destroyed by fire on 28 March 1908.

76

Ten

Queen Street

Queen Street stretches from Market Place towards the Whitehaven News offices, then turns at a right angle up to High Street, crossing Roper Street, Lowther Street and Duke Street. The lower half portion of the street is the oldest part and supposedly owes its name to Catherine of Braganza, wife of Charles II. This street had its share of public houses and warehouses, as well as fine houses for merchants, alongside the terraced houses accommodating the workers.

Lower Queen Street in 1950, with the Anchor Vaults and Lowther Arms.

A warehouse and group of workers in Queen Street, *c.* 1894.

The western side of Queen Street, leading towards Lowther Street. Only the large house at the far end of the row is still standing, the others were demolished and flats built on the site, although the three storeys are still in evidence.

No. 151 Queen Street, the house of the Gale family. A tearoom now occupies the coaching house at the back and is run by the Bonnar family.

Spooner's shop at the junction of Roper Street and Queen Street. George Kirkpatrick is the man in the foreground.

Queen Street seen from St Nicholas churchyard. The Fox and Grapes public house can be seen at No. 126 Queen Street.

A further aspect of Queen Street.

This detail of a yard off Queen Street gives an idea of what the infill housing was like. There were many small, dark areas like this one.

High Queen Street, showing houses on either side of the hill leading up to St James church on High Street. The houses were demolished in the 1960s and replaced with flats.

Eleven
Duke Street

This is the original road that led behind the Flatt Mansion and continued up to Hensingham. It can be seen on the 1642 sketch of Whitehaven. Alongside this road was a beck which flowed to the Bulwark by the harbour. The road was named Duke Street after James II when he was Duke of York.

This fine mansion was built for William Feryes, a merchant, c. 1708. The original house, called The Cupola, can be seen on the Mathias Read birds-eye view of Whitehaven from 1736. The original house had three storeys with a cupola above and a forward projecting wing on either side. There is evidence to show that the Lowthers would have preferred such a mansion to be built on Lowther Street, but William Feryes refused and built the house where he wanted it. It was altered to a two-storey property, in 1851, by architect, William Barnes.

The railings in front of the mansion are covered in snow. This view, looking towards the castle gates, shows the houses opposite the mansion.

This is the Masonic Hall, with the former health department building in the foreground, 1960s.

Somerset House was built in 1750 by Samuel Martin. He was a merchant who traded with the Americans. There have been considerable alterations to the original building. Certainly the doorway seems to be of much later date than 1750. An unusual feature of this house is the number of chimneys, some of which are visible below.

A large warehouse is pictured, with Somerset House and park in the background. This shows the direction the road used to take through the park.

Looking along Duke Street, from Somerset House towards the harbour.

A wider view of Duke Street, once again looking towards the harbour, *c.* 1900.

More shops, with the harbour in the background. These three-storied buildings would have the shop premises on the ground and the living quarters above. Has the age of the motor car arrived?

The corner of Duke Street's junction with Church Street. The Sun Inn later became the Dolphin pub and is now renamed Sal Madges. It is a popular pub run by Gordon and Betty Cottier and owned by Jenning's Brewery of Cockermouth.

Woodend's shop at No. 9 Duke Street. Pictured are Thomas Woodend with his wife and daughter Brigit in the centre, *c.* 1890.

Jackson & Murray auctioneers of No. 97 Duke Street, *c.* 1930.

The old Co-op store and Whittles furniture shop. These are situated at the junction of Duke Street and Tangier Street. The Co-op store was built in 1858 in the Italianate style which was becoming popular in Whitehaven. Whittles store was later rebuilt but still in the Italianate style. There had been buildings on these sites since the eighteenth century.

A group of shops along Duke Street, seen while looking towards the junction with Queen Street. Note the different heights, though they are each three storeys high. These were demolished during the slum clearance of the 1950s and '60s.

The Wheatsheaf Hotel stands at the corner of Duke Street and Strand Street. It is now the Paul Jones public house.

Twelve

King Street

This was the main shopping area and almost anything could be purchased from here; from drapery, furniture and clothes to pottery and crafted goods. It is worth looking at the architecture of the buildings on this street although some have been spoiled beyond redemption. King Street owes it name to Charles II who gave grants of land to Sir John Lowther. Once called the golden mile, because there was such a concentration of shops, it was said anything could be purchased in King Street. Lowther Street enjoyed the wealth in architecture and banks of the town, while King Street was the buying and selling area. The warehouses backed on to shops in Strand Street, which were developed later.

A view of King Street from the Duke Street junction, looking towards Market Place, 1930s. The view remains unchanged since the eighteenth century.

Hull's drapery shop at No. 76 King Street. This is now part of Bates Ltd, optician.

Black Lion Hotel, next to Adairs newsagents, c. 1900. A large statue of a lion stands above the first floor window.

The London and Manchester Warehouse Co. was established in 1887 at No. 22 King Street. This is now the offices of the Bradford and Bingley building society. The architecture is outstanding – notice the filias and chimneys and the decorations along the roof line.

No. 49 King Street was the premises of James Brown outfitters, c. 1910. The building now houses Benson shoe shop.

Beehive drapery shop. The Beehive traded until the 1980s when it was bought and modernised; McKays trade there now. The Beehive sign now hangs in The Beacon. It was the trademark of a woollen company and Beehive wools, knitting needles and patterns were sold in great quantity at the Beehive. This explains the large Beehive sign.

Borrowdale, tailor and draper, *c.* 1908.

Lower King Street showing Fine Fare and Roko Ltd. Pineapple public house and the market hall are in the background.

Looking up King Street towards Duke Street from Market Place. Notice the eighteenth and nineteenth-century architecture, with ornate doors and windows. Compare this with some of the unsympathetic renovations of the 1960s. Luckily not too many of the buildings underwent alterations.

A view from Lowther Street of King Street, *c.* 1910. The lady in the light coat with the basket is Mrs Summers, the wife of a local solicitor.

Thirteen
Tangier Street

In 1685 Captain Richard Senhouse purchased a large piece of land from the Brackenthwaite estates owned by Sir John Lowther. The buildings constructed on the land were built facing the sea, which came up to Tangier Street prior to the development of the harbour. A large mansion with warehouses was built with gardens; the street and mansion were named after the African settlement which was mentioned in the diary of Cathrine of Braganza – Tangiers. Later Tangier House became the property of Humphry Senhouse and was passed down through successive owners.

Waverley Hotel was once Tangier House. Originally built as a family house by Richard Senhouse, it had two forward projecting wings similar to other merchants houses, for example the YMCA in Irish Street. It was used as a Temperance House in the early part of this century and is now called the Waverley Hotel, owned and well run by Richard and Cheryl Twinn.

A parade in Tangier Street, turning into Duke Street and passing the Chusan tea room, *c.* 1900. A tremendous crowd has turned out to watch.

Gaitey cinema in Tangier Street, built in the 1920s. It was said to be the largest and most comfortable in the north of England, it was able to accommodate 1,164 people in the auditorium and 480 in the balcony. In addition it had a large café in the foyer. In 1976 it was converted to a bingo hall, though films were shown on the upper floors.

Looking towards Bransty arch. Bransty houses are visible in the background. This scene shows how busy the street was with plenty of shops, offices and pubs.

The Grand Hotel and Bransty dye works. The dye works were demolished in 1928 and the Grand Hotel burned down in January 1940.

A view towards the harbour from William Walker's offices, *c.* 1888. Theatre adverts can be seen on the hoardings.

Bransty arch was built to facilitate the transport of coal from James Pit to the harbour. The arch was demolished in 1930s, even after a 3,000 strong section of the public petitioned against it. The Grand Hotel, decorated for a celebration, can be seen in the background.

The frontage of W. Halton & Sons, printers and stationers, c. 1905. They were publishers of the *Cumberland Pacquet.*

W.R. Hinde, ships chandler and ironmonger, *c.* 1890. The man in the doorway is W. Hinde. This is now Robinson's hardware shop.

Shops in Tangier Street, c. 1900. The dental surgery is next to Turks Head Hotel and the corner of Bransty arch is visible on the right of the picture.

Bransty arch was decorated for the coronation of George V. The railway station is in the background. A horse and trap would wait here for any travellers to convey them over the short distance to the Grand Hotel.

A group of shops next to the cinema. No. 4 housed Crowther & Son woollen drapers, No. 3 was the Bluebell Inn and is now an Indian restaurant. Nos 5, 6 and 7 are now Beauty Box, Homeflair and Play and Learn, owned by Bernard Moore, whose family once owned the Beehive shop in King Street.

Dye works in Tangier Street, c. 1910. These were demolished in the 1930s to make way for the bus station. Bransty houses are visible in the background.

Fourteen
Trades and Occupations

Whitehaven's increasing prosperity in the eighteenth and nineteenth century attracted hundreds of workers into the area. Miners, carpenters, masons and sailors were all needed as the port grew in size. Extra housing was necessary as well as shops, factories and churches. In fact, information from the 1851 census on New Houses alone mentioned at least sixty different occupations, including pottery workers, tailors and hat makers. Whitehaven was the place to go in the search for full employment at this time.

Repairing nets by the shipway, East Strand in 1904.

L.H. Mclean and R.H. Charlie Pater are repairing a lobster pot on the Sugar Tongue at Whitehaven Harbour, in 1888.

This scene encapsulates the many and varied activities pursued at the harbour side during this busy period.

106

Female workers are pictured at the brickyard during World War I, probably in 1915. On the extreme right is Sarah Ann Merner and next to her is Margaret Ann Robinson.

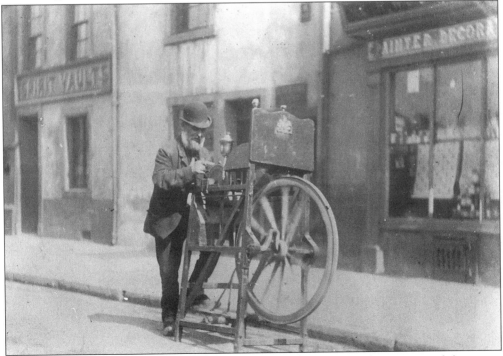

A knife grinder is at work outside the premises of Robert Woodnorth, painter and decorator, *c.* 1900.

Two men are filling a street lamp with oil outside the Whitehaven Bank, *c.* 1890. The bank was in Coates Lane at this time but later moved to Lowther Street.

Workers outside the Whitehaven Pottery, Coach Road, *c.* 1900.

Blacksmiths Arms, South Harbour, *c.* 1910. The publican was M. Brown.

The premises of Mr Hatton, printer, in Tangier Street. He printed the *Cumberland Pacquet* newspaper.

Workers at Dobson & Musgrave warehouse on West Strand, *c.* 1895.

Road men; two men with rakes tidy up surplus cobbles after relaying pavements, *c.* 1890.

Whitehaven and West Cumberland Auctioneering Co. on Preston Street. Thursday was market day when all the cattle and sheep were brought to Whitehaven to be sold. This was the nearest market for surrounding farms.

Pattinson's flour mills. This was Whitehaven's largest brick-built structure, under construction in 1907 – it was completed in 1909. It was sold and then demolished in 1975. This now forms the site of Tesco supermarket and car park.

One of the first mail vans, *c.* 1905. It has solid tyres and chain drives and a starting handle is fixed to the side. The Edward VII monogram can be seen on the side.

113

Postmen and telegram boys are pictured outside the old post office on Lowther Street, *c.* 1890.

The interior of Whitehaven laundry on Low Road, *c.* 1900. Some of the workers can be seen in the background.

Female screen workers are pictured in the canteen at William Pit, c. 1910.

Whitehaven fire brigade, July 1934. They are pictured on the secondary school playing field during a Northern District Fire Brigade competition.

The local militia and West Yeomanry were leaving the drill hall in Catherine Street to go to Lowther Castle in Penrith for Queen Victoria's funeral procession. The man looking directly at the camera is sergeant William Bell Graves.

Roan's shop, Roper Street with workers lined up outside, c. 1895.

Fifteen
Entertainment

There was plenty of entertainment in Whitehaven in the 1900s if one had the money or the time to indulge. The main sources of relaxation for men were the pubs of which there were approximately 400 even in such a small town. The women did drink ale but they sent out for it in brown jugs. There was a popular theatre in Roper Street and many of the posters advertising the acts put on there can be seen in The Beacon; some of the advertisements were printed on silk.

This cast of a theatrical show, possibly the *Mikado*, is believed to have performed at the Theatre Royal in the 1920s

Biddalls ghost show entrance, with horse-drawn show caravan to the left, *c.* 1900.

Jack Wattleworth, coal merchant, with horse and cart decorated for the coronation in either 1902 or 1911.

118

A procession by the Band of Hope marches through Market Place, before heading up Rosemary Lane to Hogarth's Mission on Mount Pleasant.

A children's tea party at Rose Hill park in 1904.

Games of marbles were played by men at Whitehaven Harbour, *c.* 1900.

This bonfire in the playground on High Street was possibly held to celebrate the opening of the playground on 13 August 1909.

G.J. Hilliard, 'The Human Anvil',
c. 1900.

Advertisement for a billiard table,
at No. 109 Queen Street, 23
February 1830.

BILLIARDS.—GEORGE JOHNSON most respectfully begs to announce to his Friends, and the Public in general, that he has erected a TABLE for the practice of that Fashionable Amusement; an accommodation which for a length of time has been much wanted in this Town.

The Table is good, and has been fitted up in a superior Manner with every requisite appurtenance, under the immediate inspection of one of the first players in the North of England.

The room is now open at his House, No. 109, Queen Street, and he trusts by paying strict Attention to the respectability of his Visitors to merit the patronage and support of those Gentlemen who many please to favour him with their company.

N.B. A private entrance to the Room up the Gateway adjoining the House.

Whitehaven, 22d February, 1830.

A REGATTA & AQUATIC SPORTS

Will be held in the
Outer Harbour, Whitehaven, on
Saturday, Sept. 13, 1919

Commencing at 12-30 p.m.

When the Sum of **£80** will be given for Prizes for the following events :

	FIRST PRIZE £ s. d.	SECOND PRIZE £ s. d.	THIRD PRIZE £ s. d.
1. Race for Fishing and Pilot Boats 28 to 40 feet overall. Handicap. Open to all comers. Triangular course about nine miles. Entrance 7/6.	£15 0 0	£7 10 0	£3 15 0
2. Race for Half Deck Sailing Boats 28 to 40 feet overall. Handicap. For Whitehaven owned vessels. Course about six miles. Entrance 3/6. Cup presented by Mr. G. Kirkpatrick, to be held by winner for 12 months. This cup will become the property of anyone winning it twice in succession or three times in all.	£11 & Cup	6 0 0	3 0 0
3. Race for Half Deck or Open Sailing Boats not exceeding 30 feet overall. Handicap. Open to all comers. Course about six miles. Entrance 3/6.	8 0 0	4 0 0	2 0 0
4. Rowing Race. Four oars. Open. Entrance 1/-.	2 0 0	1 0 0	10 0
5. Rowing Race. Two oars. Open. Entrance 1/-.	1 10 0	15 0	7 6
6. Pair Oar Sculling Race. Open. Entrance 1/-.	1 10 0	15 0	7 6
7. Mens' Swimming Race. (Scratch). Open. Distance about 200 yards. Entrance 1/-.	3 0 0	1 10 0	15 0
8. Boys' Swimming Race. 16 years and under. (Scratch). Local. Entrance 6d.	£1 & Gold Medal	15 0	Value 7/6 given by Mr. E. Lamb.
9. Ladies' Swimming Race. (Scratch). Open.	£1 & Gold Bangle.	15 0	Value 7/6 given by Mr. C. Bie.
10. Propelling Race. Competitors to propel boat by Swimming.	1 0 0	10 0	5 0
11. Shovel Race. Open to teams of Dockers & Trimmers.	1 0 0	10 0	
12. Greasy Bowsprit Walking.	A Ham.		
13. Duck Hunt.			

No Entrance Fee will be charged for Events 9, 10, 11, 12, and 13.

In Events 1, 2, and 3 the time allowance will be Eight Seconds per Foot per Nautical Mile. Four Boats to compete in each of these Events or No Race. In Events 4, 5, and 6, Three Boats to compete or No Race.

The Harbour Commissioners have kindly consented not to charge any Harbour Dues in respect of Boats entering the Harbour to Compete in the Regatta.

THE BOROUGH BAND will Play Selections of Music on the West Pier during the Afternoon.

Particulars and Entry Forms may be had on application to the Secretaries.

Entries for Events Numbered 1 to 10 (both inclusive) Close on Thursday Morning, September 11th, 1919.

J. BEATTIE,
J. SINGLETON,   Hon. Secretaries,

47 Lowther Street, Whitehaven.

Handbill for Whitehaven Regatta from 13 September 1919.

122

A merry-go-round at the fair at Whitehaven, *c.* 1906. This fair is held twice a year on the harbour side.

A bowling team is pictured outside the pavilion in Coach Road, *c.* 1910. The bowling club is still flourishing and continues to play on the same site.

PICTURE PALACE,

Market Hall,
WHITEHAVEN.

Lessee and Manager—
VICTOR BRANFORD.

Acting Manager—
JOHN WINTERBOTTOM.

7 TWICE
NIGHTLY, **9**

ALL THE YEAR ROUND.

The IDEAL and the PREMIER Picture Play House.

EDISONIA PICTURES !

The Pioneers of this Popular Form of Entertainment in the District.

Imitators we have many !
Equals we have none !! | Beautiful Pictures. Class Variety.
Charming Orchestral Music.

Whitehaven's Popular Family Resort.

| **P**eople's **P**opular **P**rices— | Tip Up Chairs, **6d.** | Body of Hall, **4d.** | Back, **2d.** |

Advertisement for the Picture Palace, in the market hall, *c.* 1912.

This is the exterior of the former onion warehouse in Swingpump Lane, behind the market hall. In later years this was converted into the Queens cinema.

THEATRE, WHITEHAVEN.
BY AUTHORITY.

FIRST NIGHT OF
PAUL JONES;
Or, Whitehaven in 1778;
WITH NEW LOCAL SCENERY, &c. &c.

ON WEDNESDAY Evening, Nov. 30, 1825, will be performed, for the first time, a New Drama, in Three Acts (written by a Gentleman of this Town) called PAUL JONES; or, Whitehaven in 1778. The Sketches of Scenery taken on the Spot by a Native Artist, and painted by Mr. DODD.

The PROLOGUE (by a Friend of the Author of the Drama) to be spoken by Mr. MUNRO.—And the EPILOGUE by Miss CLEAVER.

The following New Scenery will be exhibited :—

View at Barrowmouth, (near this Town) with the *Ranger* in the offing,

Lowther Street.

The Castle and adjacent Ground.

View of the Harbour, Shipping, &c.

The Piece concludes with a *General Conflagration,* and the retreat of the Assailants to their Vessel !

On FRIDAY EVENING a Play and Farce.

On MONDAY, Dec. 5, a Variety of Entertainments, for the Benefit of Mr. MUNRO.

CALDER BRIDGE HUNT.

THIS Meeting will take place on TUESDAY the 13th of December.

The Hounds will cast off in the Neighbourhood of

An advertisement for the first performance of the play *Paul Jones*, which was about John Paul Jones who attacked Whitehaven in 1778. This would have been seen in the *Cumberland Pacquet* of 29 April 1825.

Savages Circus proceeds through Market Place.

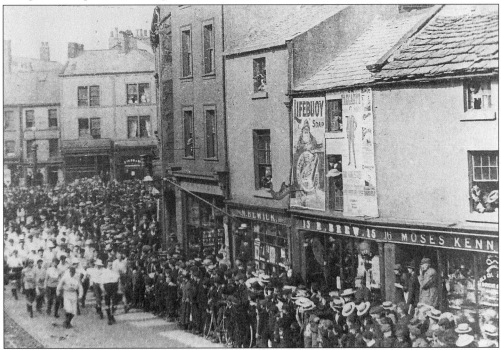

A road race passes through Market Place, *c.* 1903. The route followed the outskirts of Whitehaven, down the new road and finished at the Grand Hotel.

A seagull egg collector. Seagull eggs were used to feed the family. Note the rope that he used to climb down the cliffs.